TWIST WITH A BURGER, JITTER WITH A BUG

by Linda Lowery   pictures by Pat Dypold

Houghton Mifflin Company   Boston • New York   1995

Manufactured in the United States of America

Book design by David Saylor
The text of this book is set in 40-point Bureau Eagle Book.
The illustrations are cut-paper collages, reproduced in full color.

HOR   10   9   8   7   6   5   4   3   2   1

LIBRARY OF CONGRESS CATALOGING-IN-PUBLICATION DATA
Lowery, Linda.
Twist with a burger, jitter with a bug / written by Linda Lowery ;
illustrated by Pat Dypold.   p.   cm.
Summary: Illustrations and rhyming text provide a humorous look
at all kinds of dancing.   ISBN 0-395-67022-5
[1. Dance—Fiction.   2. Humorous stories.   3. Stories in rhyme.]
I. Dypold, Pat, ill.   II. Title.   PZ8 . 3. L955Tw   1995
[E]—dc20   93-38236   CIP   AC

Dance a mambo,

snap to a rap,

put on your cleats and tap,
tap,
tap.

Jig to the music,

sway to the tune,

polka after supper

with your fork and spoon.

Leap like a lion,

wiggle like a snake,

glide on the ice

in the middle of a lake.

Twist with a burger,

jitter with a bug,

call in the neighbors

and roll up the rug.

Hop to the rhythm,

jive to the beat,

rattle in your bones

up a DARK, DARK street.

Boogie in the bathtub,

hula-hula dance,

rumba
if you
wanna

in your
underpants.

Dance in the morning,

dance after noon,

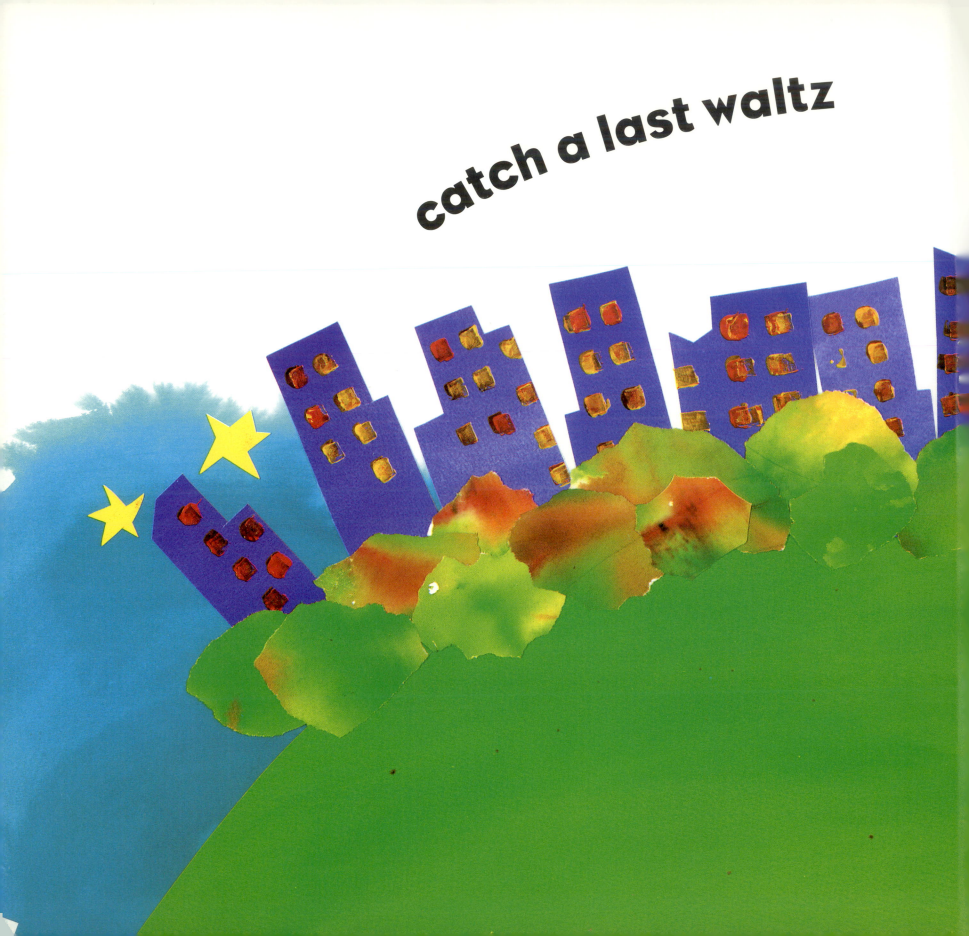

catch a last waltz

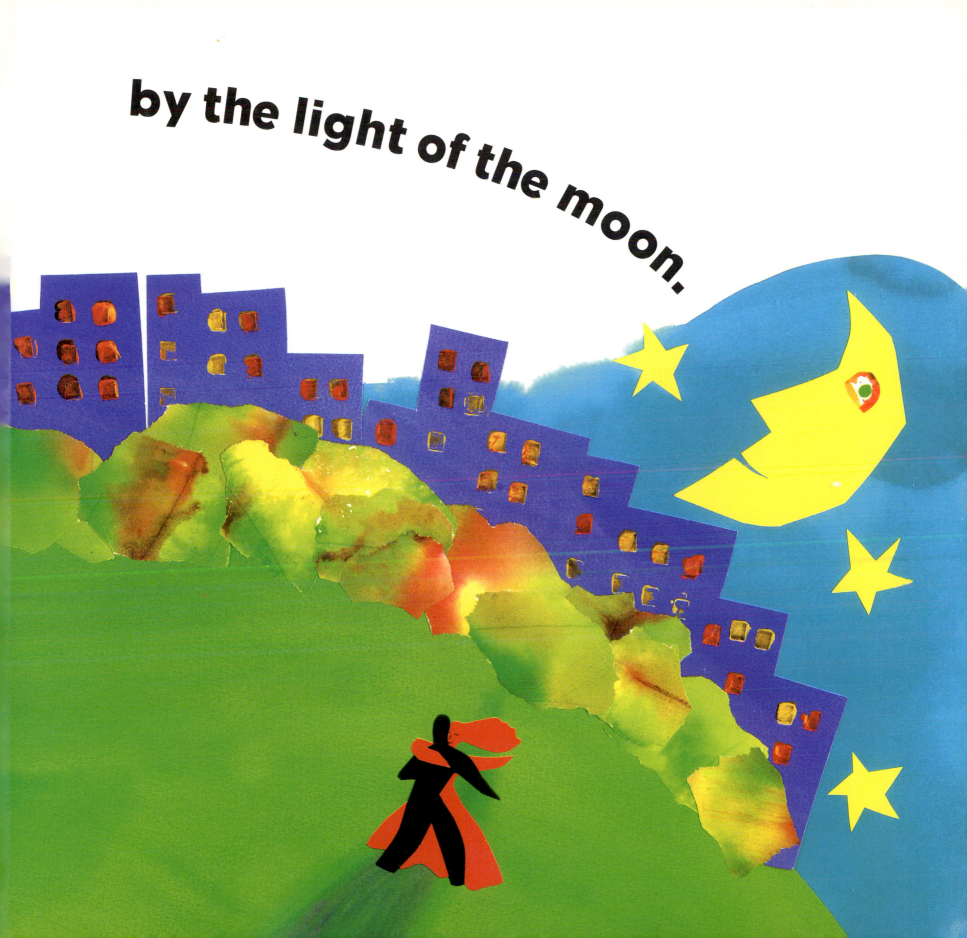

by the light of the moon.